i LOVE
what i've
forgotten

i LOVE
what i've
forgotten

Walkyria Whitlock
Illustrator: Eleyse Morgan
Editor: Erica Dansereau

lorem
PUBLISHING HOUSE

AUTHOR: Walkyria Whitlock
EDITOR: Erica Dansereau
ILLUSTRATOR: Eleyse Morgan
PUBLISHER: Lorem Publishing House Inc

Lorem Publishing House Inc
Florida

Library of Congress Control Number:
2020916321
Whitlock, Walkyria
i LOVE what i've forgotten: a novel / Walkyria
Whitlock.
p. cm.
Summary: "A simple and fun collection of poet-
ry and prose inspired by travel, love, science,
culture, and spirituality."

MOBI ISBN: 978-1-7354503-0-8
EPUB ISBN: 978-1-7354503-4-6
HARDCOVER: 978-1-7354503-1-5
PAPERBACK: 978-1-7354503-2-2
AUDIOBOOK: 978-1-7354503-3-9

Printed on demand nearest to you.

www.lorempublishinghouse.com

thank you to everyone, for everything.

for you

contents

acknowledgements

Forever astounded by the wonder of life, first and foremost, thank you God for this incredible journey and for bringing this book to life.

Thank you to all of my family and friends. Your support, love, and simple presence in my life means everything. I love you.

Thanks to my mom, Sophie, who has sacrificed everything for my brother and me.

Thanks to my brother, Kaleb, who inspires me in the most bountiful and peculiar ways.

Thanks to my grandparents, Majo and Tollan, whose support has provided ongoing stability and inspiration in my life.

Thanks to both of my dads, Steve and Tim, whose roles in my life have been truly impactful and inspired my growth.

A very special thanks to Erica, Ellie, and Tyler, whose patience and diligence were absolutely fundamental in putting this work together.

To the many people who have helped me over the years in many ways, I hope to live as graciously and generously as you. Thank you.

preface

Dear Reader,

Here is my love letter to you. I hope this book simply enhances your life. If you are going through good times, I hope it helps you to realize your treasures. If you're going through bad times, I hope you find comfort through this, realizing that you're not alone and things get better.

Your presence in this world is absolutely necessary. You are a part of a grand work of art, and you have great significance! I feel so honored that you have chosen to read my book. I truly hope that you enjoy it, but most importantly, I hope that you enjoy your life. It is truly so special.

Stay proactive in your joys and focus on the good.

Your hopeful romantic writer,

Walkyria

introduction

the one line illustration is a reflection of what a single stream of consciousness can create and a reminder to stay hopeful when life throws you for a loop.

set your surroundings for romance and peace. take in these words like the smell of pink roses on a saturday market in france.

read these pages with your own divine confidence.

dreams are not always what they seem. between the shining moments often live heartbreak, failure, seemingly unending questions, and pinched pennies... these are call to action moments where you are challenged to grow deeper in faith, hope, and love. it is greater faith, hope, and love that is needed to achieve our dreams.

every experience refines us. long before i knew God, someone told me: "perhaps God has better plans for you than you could ever make for yourself." it has stuck with me and is so true. though life may bring you moments of pain and uncertainty, i hope these words inspire your spiritual journey as you connect with some of the ups and downs of my own life.

a human experience
containing contradictions,
multitudes, and varying levels of
depth
through a single thread of being

page one

you can read a whole
book of my thoughts
but i will sum it up in a
single sentence that i
did not create:

life is beautiful.

j u s t   begun
around mountains
around rivers
around bends
you knew you'd find it
but you didn't know when

along the way
too many say
you've made it
but to the heights you're going
you've only just begun

ocean blues
like jazz and muse
down in new orleans
you haven't sought
though somehow you've caught
wonders yet to be seen

along the way
too many say
you've made it
but to the heights you're going
you've only just begun

twinkle
twinkle dee
twiddle dough
i'm on an island
and stubbed my toe

from playing kids' games
running too fast
not paying attention
i wanted love to last

live
how has life shaped and molded
you?
are you who you want to be?
did you sit back and watch the
process?
or did you participate actively?

can you say that your dreams were
followed?
and in the end, you were all you
found?
can you say that you are happy
when the room is empty, no one
around?

peace
         peace
peace
peace of your mind

start right now and live how you
want to
it's not too late to dream some-
thing new
hoist your sails and now you're
gliding
the adventure is your dream come
true

faith
hope
love
it's all coming true

I don't know anything

I'm far less open to things I think
I know
Than to things that I don't get

But the more I'm open to what
I know
The more experience that I get
The more experience that I get

And the more experience that I get
The more I realize I don't know

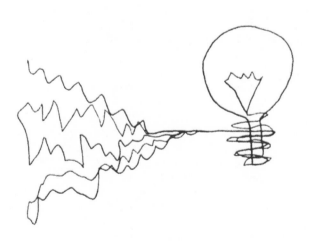

f r e e
how the wind dances with trees
making their music
forcefully inviting all that are free
to join in

i want to join...
my hair does
but i am too bound
beyond my realization
to join in the dance of the wind
more bound than a tree
odd

i allow my dress
to float around me as my own secret
detest
for i will not be free

friday night l i g h t s

and at this moment

i relate to the friday night spot–
lights

whose search in the night sky is
endless

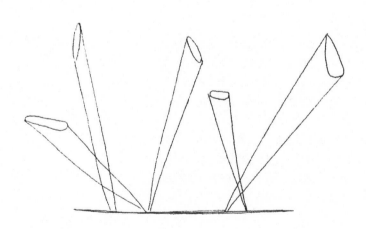

a feeling
when something lights your path
you can see the way
the strings of uncertainty simply dissipate
nothing holds you back
as you stride towards a place you know is true
and you rejoice on your same path
knowing
something
guides you

though the light may flicker
dim
or even
disappear
you do not feel uncertain
as you know that
now
you are near
to the place you knew existed
and the light that beckons you
a calling from the distance
finally coming into view

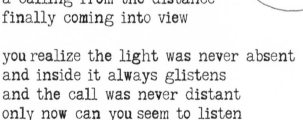

you realize the light was never absent
and inside it always glistens
and the call was never distant
only now can you seem to listen

there was never a destination
nor a path or a mission
simply a feeling as you stepped
and how the ground
met against your sole.

j u s t   for   u s

beautiful
beautiful
beautiful
beautiful and loving
beautiful and loving
beautiful and loving
beautiful and loving and kind
beautiful and loving and kind
beautiful and loving and kind
beautiful and loving
and kind and just
and kind and just
and kind and just
just for us
yes just for us

the endless desert
magic, harsh, unforgiving
momentary bliss

female of the times
my time is remarkable
i don't let the good times merely
pass

my time is unforgettable
i do what i can to make love last

i am a woman confused
by my
inspirational
ties

i know that i am one
all i know is i am one

why should i refine you and i
YOU
AND
I
YOU AND I

i am a female of my time
i am a female with a sharp mind
i am a female
or am i
because i am cold

i am a female of the times
i am broken
i am strong
i am fine

i drink a little bit of wine
oh I'm just a female of the times
do you feel my broken touch
do you feel my broken touch
because i am fierce
and i am frightened
by my own mind

and i feel the comfort of the
rhymes
wondering
if i was not beautiful
would i be able to make a beautiful
sound
would my inspiration be pure
how would i be sure
that nothing's wrong with me
if i wasn't always accepted
always for my beauty

oh don't you see
i know my heart is true
but if i was a true female of the
times
i would not mind
how i am drugged to be
a beautiful rug

oh i am sure
i can be cured
but i cannot feel
like i cannot heal

i cannot heal if i cannot feel
oh am i real if i don't even feel

oh to be real
i must feel

i cannot block any pieces of me
or i will not be me

oh real
how real
how real is it to feel
is to be
is to love
is it to touch

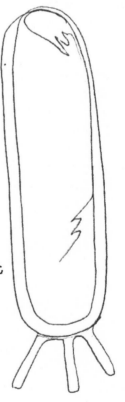

i hope that you are not broken yet
because i can't bear
this feeling
this feeling
bear this feeling
that i'm dreaming
alone

skylight
i used to think about this all of the time
but this
this is not what I had in mind
this is not what my dreams are about
this is not where we figure it all out

i used to think about this all of the time
but this
this is not what I had in mind
there is no desire in my heart
i think this means that it's time for us to part

because what brings us together
is what tears us apart

this is not what my dreams are of
moody skylight from up above

DIRECTION
love what you love
give what you can
at the end of the day
it's all in God's hands

you may feel like running
but you cannot flee
have faith hope and love
what will be will be

so stand in your essence
all will value your presence
knowing that divine connection
is your only direction

Let each obstruction
Be pronounced
As another
Point of beauty
To reflect
More light

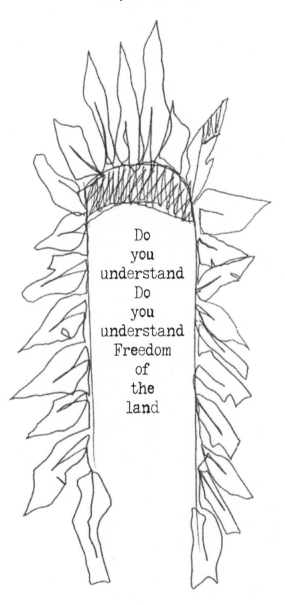

Do
you
understand
Do
you
understand
Freedom
of
the
land

Freedom of the land

i n the END
sometimes it's smooth
sometimes it's rough
there are parts
that flow aimlessly together
sometimes there are parts
that seem to be separated
from the rest
but at some point
it all comes together
there are straightaways
and waves
then there are the random kinks
there are highlights
in bad days
and good ones
it can be long
it can be short
but it is always beautiful
and in the end
it's just hair.

rapture
what a delight
to live by light
not by sight
or fear of night
but soulful spright
and all that's right
what a delight
to live by light

j u s t   be
the only thing i have
i'm not even guaranteed
and sometimes i forget to take
the only thing i need

truth be told it's not that hard
but i am sick of being scarred
all these cuts upon my knees
i started to think my only job was
to please

so whatever it is you have to say
save it for another day
because i am here to sing
and dance and play

oh what it is to be free
what it is to be me
what it is to be free
what it is to just be

it's such a strange world
full of deceit
it's such a strange world
full of defeat

but the deceit and defeat
we alone bring to life

only YOU
the thing about vulnerability is that it's all relative

only you know what puts your nape at the edge of a
knife and sends shudders down your spine as you cling
to your words like they were your life... taking every
last ounce of air before exasperating yourself almost
to the point where it would be too late to let them go
and you let them go
only you know the relief...
the weight that's given way
the clean air that suddenly surrounds you
the clearing in your mind
the depth
the clarity

only you

only you know the growth that comes from letting
those fears go and facing the world raw and whole
those vulnerabilities become a point of strength
and before you know it,
speaking of them is no longer a feat for you

but only you know this

people on the other side will admire your strength, and
you may inspire them to find their own

but you will grow stagnant if you do not face your
next vulnerability
your next scare
your next fear
that layer that you hold onto for comfort or strength
or perhaps because you do not know it is there

only you will know when it is time to let it go

only you can let it go

such a heartless q u e e n
so it seems so it seems
she's a heartless queen
so it seems

oh her lover let her down
he's not around
he's not around
oh her lover let her down
he's not around

he's nowhere to be found
they looked around
but he let her down

she's dreaming like a queen
but she won't wear the crown
because he let her down

so a heartless princess was found
a heartless princess was found

then one day he came back around
she's bitter now
because he let her down
still she took the crown

but she wears a frown
because he let her down
she let herself grow mean
and thus lives the heartless queen

GROW
what have we forgotten?
and will we ever know?
all the spaces left behind
are giving room for us to grow
grow
grow
grow grow grow
grow

HELLO
hello
hello
sweet child
welcome to the world

it starts with me
frolicking in the flowers
it starts with you
learning the ways of the sea

to the edge of the world
we travel
we see

and i see white dresses
and i see long tresses

it started with me
it started with you

oh we welcome the new to the world
finally i understand
it starts with you
it starts with me

abandonment

it creates such a unique atmosphere

bliss

abandoned buildings
full of overgrown plants and strays
vibrant with life
living and giving

here it stands
welcoming all
a statement to those who left it

beauty:
anything that excites a greater
appreciation for life

BUTTERFLY

like a butterfly
she flutters about
and you are mesmerized by her
waiting for the moment she will stop for you

perhaps she lands on you ever so lightly
her interest fades quickly
as you see the detail in her intricate wings
you know she will leave soon
and you allow it

you know inherently
that touching her will mean her losing part of herself
as she is not free without her flight

you bask in the luck that she chose to land on you
when you were younger
you would've tried to capture her in your foolishness

but she means more to others than she does to you
them tokening her with too much beauty
too much symbol

yet you agree she does live grandly
she knows that her life will be shorter than yours
and you fear for her delicacy
but you do not fear for when she appears to drop
as this is part of her dance with the world as she flies
freely

in her haste
she will lose you
but it is okay
because those that capture
kill the butterfly

what's this
am i finding
beauty
am i finding
beauty

in fact
all i see
is you and me

but

am i finding
beauty

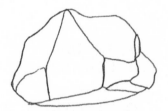

smooth tiger
i've been told i glow before
you've been told that too
for i have never seen a glow
quite like you

s c a r s
not that you'd understand
but the pain has made me
who i am

old wounds
they heal
but the scars
they still

are seen
daily

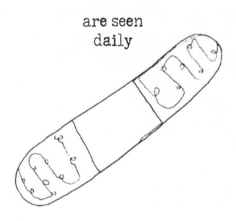

insecurities? i have a few!
issues? i've got them too!
not all of them i care to show
my friends and family--they sure know
my best guess is you've got them too
from what i have learned, we all do
the more you accept and express
the less likely you will repress
and from there, you will grow and thrive
focused on the joy to be alive

i once saw a fortune teller, and he asked me
what i wanted to see in my future. i told him
that i wanted my life to be magical. he whis-
pered and said, "it already is."

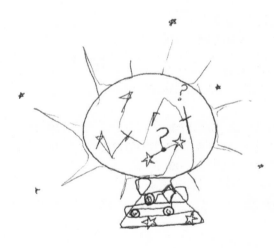

o p e n   door

my soul wanders as much as my mind
they say hurry up, but i take my time
no need to move forward, no need to rewind
let me feel the beauty
the whole world is blind

shuffle my thoughts
shuffle my intentions
my motive is questioned
by my shifting attention
and they all say that i lack direction
oh i follow the path of my intuition

fear holds me no more
i live life with an open door

        fear holds me no more
        i live life with an open door

        on this journey to share my light
        my heart is not burdened by mortal fright
        my eyes will be open
        but i will lose sight
        my soul always knows what direction is right

        blindly struck
        i'll never know it
        vulnerable and innocent
        i try not to show it
        though my instincts are likely to blow it
        the seeds have been planted
        it's time to sow it

        fear holds me no more
        i live life with an open door

process of the light
we must learn not to fight
we must learn to unite
it won't happen overnight
trust the process of the light

SEASONS

i used to think of you in the summertime
oh but now you'll never know
i used to think of you in the summertime
oh how the seasons come and go

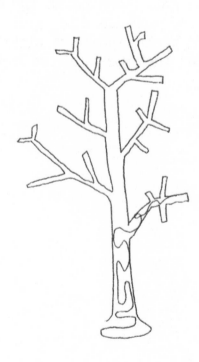

balance

let there be
good and bad
light and dark
hot and cold
as contrast allows us to see and appreciate
the magnificence of our preference.

sometimes the purpose of an obstruction is to amplify

listen

UP AHEAD
you see
you see your life go down
and you believe
you believe
it's over now

you make–believe
that it's over now
so you don't have to care anymore
so you don't have to care
so you don't have to bear anymore
so you don't have to bear

but can you see the lights up above
and can you reach
what is above you
oh you keep on flying by memories
and keep your spirit high
as high as you can reach

i can see
i can see
that you want to go
i'm full of visions from up ahead
and
you're not even close to being dead
stop filling your mind with dread
you've got beauty up ahead.

w i t h   you
does it seem real to you?
because i can see
all of your beauty
yes i can see
all of your beauty

does it seem true to you?
that the divine
is here all of the time
speaking through you
does it seem true?
does it seem real to you?
can you feel it too?
i know that
i feel your wounds

you can stop where you are or
you can keep going—you'll go far
just know that I am here with you
just know that I am here with you

happy
i won't tell you who to be
i just want you to be happy

on the way you may struggle
just know that i'll be here to cuddle

yeah you might lose your way
just know that i'm going to say

i just want you to be happy
i just want to see that smile on your face
i just want you to be happy
i'll help you find happiness in this place

i won't tell you where to go
but i'll show you places that i know
you might find you like a few
but to thy own self stay true

on our journeys come what may
maybe one day i'll hear you say

i just want you to be happy
i just want to see that smile on your face
i just want you to be happy
i'll help you find happiness in this place

they say it's not where you are
it's always who you're with
just know
that i can't
think of a better person to be with

let's   p r e t e n d
oh you
your heart is mending

and i
i am defending

oh you
you are descending

and i
i am pretending

that
you and i
are not ending

oh i'm just pretending

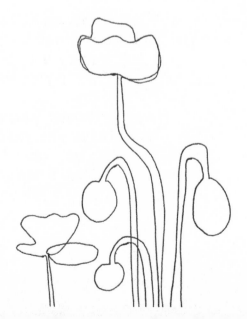

walkyria whitlock

i am not afraid for i see nothing that
hasn't been touched by light

DREAM

dream because you can
it will color your life
adding hope, wonder, and purpose
it will comfort your soul
giving it direction, aim, and focus

but don't just dream

DO

because you can
you can turn your dreams into reality
you owe it to the world
to make something beautiful
come to life

do it for others
to show them what hard work
and dedication can achieve
to inspire, to relate

anything is possible
the world is a law of pure potentiality
and you better believe it

BELIEVE

because YOU CAN.

in the fields
beating true
feeling new
swinging around
feet off the ground
holding my hand
trusting no plan
so we hold tighter
for a little longer
the future looks brighter
i hope we grow stronger

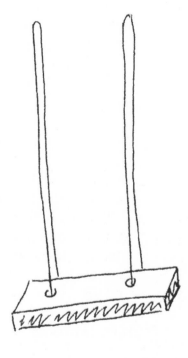

HUSH
i can see it now
i paint the prettiest of pictures
when i'm in the greatest pain
yes my life has a lot of sunshine
but there's been a lot of rain
rain to keep the plants giving
rain to keep my spirit lush
i don't know why i keep my pain
so hush hush

so hush hush

i'm not battling my demons
i'm not falling in their game
i just don't know how to receive them
and understand what is their aim
perhaps they are not demons
just a chisel
and i'm the stone
they're simply helping to shape me
into the sculpture i'll soon become

soon become.

We were
      fairies

            dancing

      in the
            night

      Riding
            on ribbons

                  of moonlight

p i c k e d
sometimes
i feel like a dandelion

a flower
that flourishes like a weed

picked
by the simple-minded as a weed,
by the simple-hearted as a flower,
and
by the ones who go deep—to the
roots,

for healing

If we give the most focus to
the things that bring peace
and joy then that is the direc-
tion the world will go.

holding tightly
letting go
waiting for signs
that time will show
piece it together
we may fall apart
life isn't easy
with a wandering heart

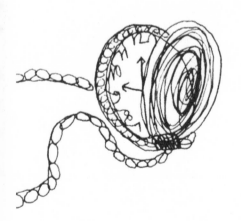

shade on me
insecurities released
because i don't need that shade on me
yeah i don't need that shade on me

and while the world is passing by
no one can understand why
why oh why
there's no shade on me

you're the sparkle in my eye
perhaps you're the reason why
why
oh why
there's no shade on me

PROCESS
you'll figure it out
what life's about
there is not a map you can use
there is not a dictionary to understand
there is not a single way for anyone
there's just a single way for you

you'll figure it out
what life's about

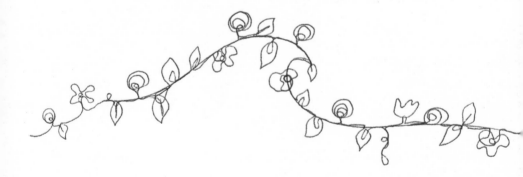

maybe i'm in the land of yesterday
or tomorrow
i couldn't say

maybe i'm in the land of yesterday
or tomorrow
it's all the same

stardom
she was a star
perhaps a small one
that no one really noticed

perhaps without any orbiting planets

but

a star

nonetheless

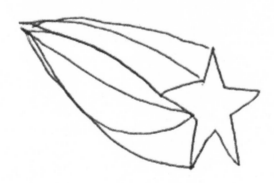

the whole world around you is
simply love or lack thereof
fill any empty space you see
with love and watch as the
world blossoms around you

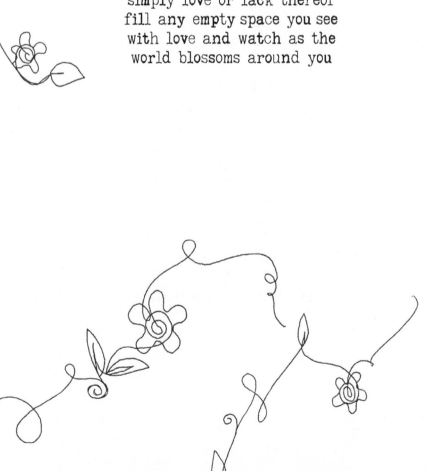

You are my Sun

today is always the day
and now

always the moment
that i will love you

for you
there is no blue
no grey
just the sun
and its hidden rays

the colors are merely of the sun
the source of all energy
from a collective one

at night
it leaves its reflection in the moon
as the sun
will never leave us
lightless
but i thank
YOU
for all the brightness

I LOVE YOU
i love to see your joy
i love to watch you smile
i love to see your face light up when i see you after a
while

i love to share in your excitement
i love to cheer on your success
i love that even when i am not there i feel connected
nonetheless

i love when you are happy
but i want to be there when you're stressed
i want to be the one who reminds you: it's okay, you are
blessed

i want you to know this
and i know you know i'm talking to you
because you're everyone i've ever loved or ever knew

l a y e r s
when you realize your mind is not you
nor is your body
or your past

you realize that given the
mind
body
and past
of someone else

you would make the exact same decisions
leading the same path
the same life

and thus through our core
through the truth
the essence
we are connected infinitely in each and every moment

abyss
when
you
look
at
the
sky
at night,

do
you
only
notice
the dark abyss

or

the
twinkling stars?

p l a y g r o u n d
if you start to recognize how magical you
are
then naturally you'll see it in the people
around you

and then the whole world will turn into
this magical playground
that you get to call

home.

acutely sensitive
to the fleeting nature of being alive.

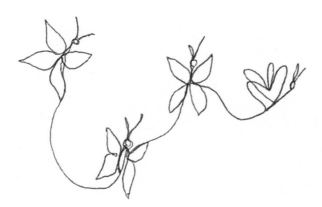

The
best
way
to
make
the
world
a
better
place
is
to
help
others
believe
in
the
good
of
it.

f i j i
the birds are brighter
the smiles are whiter
weeds are free to grow

my fire is burning
so much i'm learning
and so much i'll never know

adieu
i don't understand my own reasons
for what i choose to do
i don't understand the things that i'm fighting
or if i'm fighting to get back with you

oh why

why did i choose this way

why

please tell me it is okay

far off from letting go of you
i have let go of my things
but i wonder if they are still at your house
or if you threw them out

i guess if i was in your position
i would have done the same
i want to hope that you'll think of me
in the nice ways, without pain

i hope you realize you still visit me
when i sleep
i look in your eyes

and i realize
i don't understand my own reasons
for what i choose to do
but i know there are grander reasons
so i bid you adieu

he calls wanting h e r back
no

you were right

i would've lost myself loving you
and i would've forgotten the rest of the world

i never would've impacted so many lives
i never would've seen myself in this light

i lost you before i was myself
and i do thank you for that

for a bud cut too soon
leaves more nutrients for blossoms to grow

it has not happened yet
but your memory will be replaced
it has not happened yet
but your memory will be erased

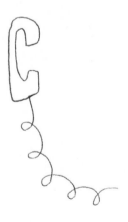

alone so far up

i prayed for rain as i drowned in the clouds
never minding the signs to come down
come down

as the rain poured down
flooding the lands beneath me
finally i could breathe

but there was no ground for me to land on
so i stayed in the sky
filling the clouds as i would cry

alone so far up
i pray for rain
just so i can breathe

k i n d
beauty is eternal
the spirit is divine
happiness is fleeting
truth less important
than to be kind

YOU
your beauty is in the way you see
how you look with care and deeply

your strength is in the way you walk
like nowhere you've ever been has held you back

your grace is in the way you speak
with words that uplift me when I am weak

but far more than anything that i can see
is close to what you mean to me

not a butterfly at all
she discovered
she was not a butterfly at all
sure her wings would catch her
when she would fall

but she was not a butterfly at all
touch would not hurt her
her wings were strong

a swift breeze
taken with ease
no, she was not a butterfly at all

if there was a word
you might use
it would be
angel

yes, she was not a butterfly at all
she was much greater
she was an angel

san francisco
something to look up to
something to look forward to
something i can chase

parked on top of potrero hill
living in my car
having a movie night
i lay awake
i lay awake

lost in the hills
on the hills of san francisco

revolution
we all want to believe in the imaginable
soon it will be cold enough to build fires
we must hope the fire only keeps us warm
and does not consume us

abalone
i watch you
unwavered
by the tide
that moves
high and low
whose low times
have killed
many around you

but you startle
by the slightest change
in scenery
if you suspect
something new

something new
that's what
scares you

it's just
something new

and you don't know what to do

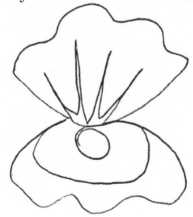

rolling stone
i don't want to go down a hill
simply for a thrill

tell me what rock starts to climb

okay
i know so little about so much
i know so much about so little

life's riddle

a beauty
a pain

you are human
it's okay
you are human
you'll make it through another day

you are human
you know the way
you are human
it's okay

you do you
but this is me
this is me
this is me

you can hold onto your fears

i'm setting mine free
i'll set them free
i'll set them free

create your fire
but let me be
let me be
let me be

if stars align
then i will see
finally
i will see

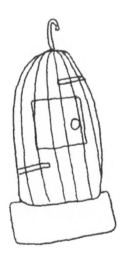

this is me
and i am free
you set me free
finally

believe in love and
what it brings
so i'll do me
you'll see
you'll see

your fears cage you
but i'll do me
oh i'll do me
for eternity

h e a r joy
life's a journey
and down the road
i will grow old
but i'm on the run

a rolling stone
collects no moss
but it's only going
down the hill

what happens
when the hill stops
will you grow roots?
so you can see the treetops?

or would you rather grow wings?
and pray that your loved ones all
sing?
so you may hear of the joys their life
brings

magician
magic
is in our perception

like a magic show

there are different roles

you can choose to be in awe
or pick things apart

what role will you play?
someone who watches unphased
or is simply amazed

or will you, my friend

become the magician?

perhaps it is the pessimist
that is
actually naive.

rock–a–bye

you say you don't believe in
god
but you say you know love

oh everyone has their own
way
but everyone can learn how
to pray
it's not about what you say
it's about what you feel
and giving thanks

you say
you believe in God
but you don't feel
you just don't feel
i know like you've gotten enough
everyone
everybody will be okay
you believe in God
oh isn't that enough
you say that you believe in we want the whole world
God but we've already got it
oh but you have a mind full
of fear of what's to come
you think that you've
you've seen it all
oh everyone has their own but you cannot see how
way small
but everyone can learn how how small we are
to pray and we're just a part
it's not about what you say yeah you
it's about what you feel you don't see where you are
and giving thanks

oh everyone
everyone
i know everyone
everyone has their own way
everybody will be okay yeah and everyone
everyone
everyone
is going to be okay
i see love, hope. and faith

great cost

i have pranced and danced
and long romanced
of places i never knew
i have bargained and fiddled
and sometimes belittled
people i thought i outgrew
but now that i've traveled
now that i've grown
now that i've been
all on my own
more than a little
i've missed and i've lost
time with my loved ones
what a great cost

how can you speak to me of how i should fly

if you have not flown?

```
l e o
```
a lion stands so mighty

but what makes a lion, a lion?
is it the fierceness in its roar
the sharpness of its teeth
the fear it could instill
the respect demanded sheerly through its presence?

no.

it is the courage in its heart
the strength of its character
the warmth of its purr
the honor of its spirit

and thus a beast can reside in any character
be its will

but the essence lies not within any movement or mo—
tion but simply what it is

in stillness.

nora
why
wouldn't
everything
be
beautiful
in
our

imaginations?

big b a n g
a flash of expansive
endless
light
created the universe

the light
could've
lasted forever
in fact
it does
infinitely so
it grows
and expands

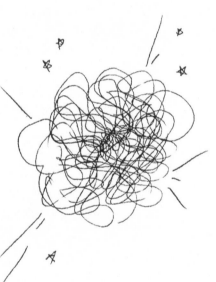

light
has dispersed
everywhere
and darkness
created
so you
could take form

the darkness
is nothing more
than an outline
that helps
define the shape
of light

it is possible
indeed
that darkness
does not exist
but is simply
a form of light
our eyes
do not recognize

walkyria whitlock

relativity
no one really knows
where they are going
so with no point of reference
you never really know where you are

if we spend
our lives
looking at our watches
we will end up
going in circles

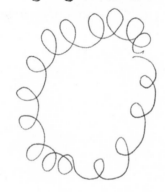

metamorphosis
a butterfly comes from darkness
as does the sprout of a flower and a newborn
perhaps darkness is not what we think it is
perhaps it is simply a safe place to grow

like a caterpillar
encompasses itself
into darkness
the mind encases itself
to transform

all things beautiful are magical

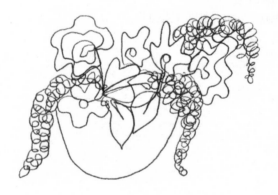

Eunoia
Fall in love
With each and every moment
Each breath
Each passing glance
Each touch
Hold on to each moment
For their time
And as they leave
Let them go
Welcome the new passing moment

Let yourself be amazed
Hold your breath
Just for the thrill
Of catching it again
Hold hands
Be close
Be excited
To experience this life
Cherish it
Cherish your life and others

Be patient
Be kind
Accept and rejoice
Have faith and hope
And love
Because there is no other way.

hypothesis
what we don't know
and could never prove
we can assign truth
and upon the belief
of that truth
and action
it becomes real

relate
through music
i strike the eye of a blind man
through pictures
i strike the heart of a deaf man
through words
i just try to describe them

a visual spritzer

an evening run
back to the marina
dark
metallic
electric tonic
harbored endorphins
serene harbor

the water tickles my hands
in my thoughts

it cleanses my heart
with its gentle stir

and in my own stillness
wrapped by its wavering nature
it releases the weight in my feet

i feel fluid and

one with the world.

compassion
gives
life
flavor

a   h o m e
pull my hands away
i feel the shudder
as i close another door
i look around
a familiar clutter
it seems that i've been here before

i guess it's time i started cleaning
though not all the mess is mine
one moment lost
then somehow forgotten
i found things i never thought i'd
find

i found a home
a home
in the heart of the divine

birdie

i look up
and you look down
i learned to fly
and you shot me down
i believe in what i say
you learned to lie
and you walked away
you walked away
away
with a crooked smile
and cheating ways
you walk away
away
and i'm a stupid girl
for wanting you to stay

you walked out
and i lucked out
not sure what good
i saw now

because i accepted
all your harm
you will not suffer
a single scar
and you walk away
away
with a crooked smile
and cheating ways
you walk away
away
and i'm a stupid girl
for wanting you to stay
you will learn the hard way
now
i learned i cannot teach you
how
but now i must fix
my wings
though they may be broken
i can still sing
ladada ladada
and i'm a stupid girl
for wanting you to stay

no matter what
she sees smiles
and feels people's laughter
he counts the miles
not sure what he's after

but they find each other

she radiates
all of the possibilities
he followed them once
now unhappy with where they lead

but they find each other

he is so daring and planning ahead
she just wants him to stay in her bed

but they find each other
yes no matter what
one day

they find each other

and he brings her to see a new
view
and she brings him to see a view
like it's new
yes
he needed sunshine
she needed his divine

and
   through

       the

                bro k e n n e s s

        all   i   can

                          see

      is
            love

the sea
my feet in the sand
i welcome
constant crashing
oh the thrashing
of the sea

i hear the noise
and feel the water
it's low tide
no one
by my side
with the sea

and every second
it goes away
away from me
away from me
the sea

and every second
i see the sea
it comes to me
it comes to me
the sea

it drowns the time
like it drowns the sand
i need no plan
i need no land
with the sea

a beautiful mind
i'd like a beautiful being
to be with me
and play with me
in the sea

the moment is now
and the sky is clear
i hold no fear
my conscience clear
with the sea

friendship b l e s s i n g s
live life
live long
hold my hand
we'll be strong
be real
stay true
and know
that i couldn't live my life
without you

en ad

i know that life will bring you
beautiful things

i hope i am
one of those
things that it brings

oh what will it bring

        what will it bring

they
see
me
rolling
down the street

BANG
BANG
BANG

my bike's backfiring

breeze
the wind whispers
that you
are something greater
than you can even see

the wind whispers
because she knows more
than your mind
could dream to explore

oh
the wind
she whispers
to me

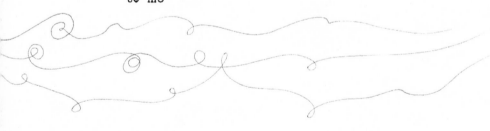

we
are
all just
waiting

we are just
waiting

for the light

to shine

on our path

i am learning
that if i
want to change
the shape
of anything in life
i need to touch it
i need to feel it
i need to warm it up
with my soul
then it becomes malleable
in my hands
like clay.

here
i am young
i am free

am i where
i'm supposed to be?

i think so
i think so

i like roaming
through the streets

smiling at strangers
that i greet

warms my soul
warms my soul

and the sun
it tans my feet

i know i'm where
i'm supposed to be

here is home
here is home.

the shoreline
which wavers
back and forth
is still
somewhat defined
and she was sure
she would never be as shore
as the edge
of the ocean

yolo

oh
this
is
a
beautiful
life
and
we
don't
get
to
live
it
twice

and
that
is
something
so
special

your beautiful life
never happens twice

ashes

completely open
yet still ashamed
i bare my soul
to an open flame

the fire grows
at my expense
and the ashes
i cannot dispense

yet i understand
ashes on my hands
i have given
similar demands

we all do it
we all say
that for someone else
we know a better way

no smoke in our eyes
we turn to ash
the pieces of
another's life

with the window open
we try to vent
to clear the smoke
it feels distant

clearer judgment
with our clear eyes
unable to understand
why they feel compromised

fan the smoke
then kill the flame
our pyro hearts
have grown bored of this game

we all do it
we all say
that for someone else
we know a better way

no smoke in our eyes
we turn to ash
the pieces of
another's life

oh ashes ashes
ashes
we
all
fall
down

i lost myself for a minute
and now i'm just getting back in it
what's my limit

i have no limit
no limit
no limit

all i know
she says
i am an artist
and i will continue
to explore this

as i know that
i love what i love

she says
i am an artist
and i will continue
to explore this

even as i grow old

oh my art
where did it start?
and where
will it take me?

oh i am expressing
my heart through art
and that's simply
all i know

she says
i am an artist
and i will continue
to explore this

through this lens

she says
i am an artist
and i will continue
to explore this

until my life ends

oh my art
where did it start?
and where
will it take me?

oh i am expressing
my heart through art
and that's simply
all i know

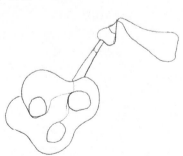

a n c h o r e d
i hear the music
from ashore
i came to explore
but i am anchored at sea
oh how can this be

am i doing what i should
am i living how i should
am i dreaming how i should
am i believing in the good
oh
what am i doing
who am i with
what am i being
do i exist

am i real
is it real
what i feel

oh what am i doing
here
when i want to be
part of the music
part of the music
part of the world

i see all the buildings
illuminated by the light
i hear the water crash
it is night
and i want to be ashore
because i came to explore

i came for so much more
oh just let me go ashore

am i dreaming
is this my life
am i living
is this just night

oh what am i doing
who am i with
what am i being
does this exist

am i real
am i real
am i real
am i real

objectified
what am i
in a man's eyes
nice legs thick hips
and thighs
i think he's going to love me
and then he
he doesn't want me

what am i
in a man's eyes
soft skin soft lips
big eyes
i think he
he really sees me
but i just look pleasing

what am i
in a man's eyes
should i even be surprised
am i a compromise
am i a compromise

am i compromised

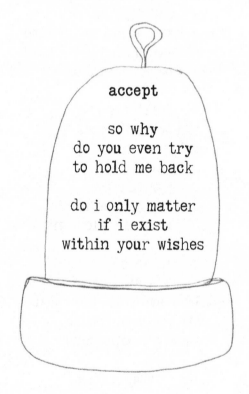

accept

so why
do you even try
to hold me back

do i only matter
if i exist
within your wishes

l u n a lullabies
mars is lighting up the sea tonight
oh and i believe something is going
right

i believe
i believe
in lunar lullabies

i believe
the moon is full of surprises
for you
and me

the sea and stars
so very special
stars are falling
all around
it seems the sky is finally awake

listen to me
singing lunar lullabies

you must endure the night
if you are to know what is right
to know light

look at the stars
they bring insight

and no matter what you say

or do

i'll bring light to you

i'll bring light to you

seeing is believing

there are so many dimensions

if we can dream it

that means we can see it

if we can see it

might as well believe it

believe in your dreams

little birdies
singing in the garden
imagine we could join them

we would all start to sing
and then we would spread our wings
and then
                we
                would
                start
                to fly

sleep peacefully
     d r e a m heavenly

there's still a whole
     world out there for you to see

empty
living in an empty bed
thoughts of you
creep into my head

i don't think i fit
in an empty bed
unless thoughts of you
thoughts of you

fill my head.

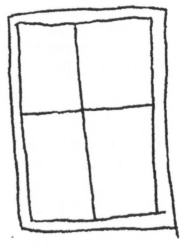

je m'en fous
i can stare
looking out the window
all day
wondering what the people
passing by would say

do they see me
peering at them
what do they think

do they think
i need some help
should i see a shrink

but i continue
continue
continue
to stare

cause i don't really care
je m'en fous

who are you?
where do you want to go?
who do you want to be?
what do you believe?
what do you believe?
do you even know?

i know.

i was a waterfall
down by the ocean
and you could hear my roar
if only you dared
to explore
if only you dared
to explore
you could be more

what you become
has so much to do
with what you release

what you release
has so much to do
with what you believe

what do you believe?

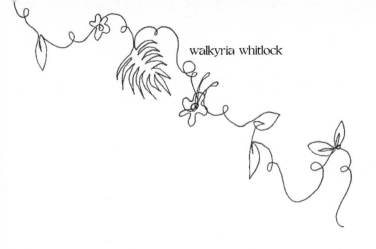

walkyria whitlock

through the lens of love
we can see beauty in everything

so much of
    freedom
        is simply

  about

not having

  your

    mind

       enslaved

the secret
daisies, lilacs, poppies too
wildflowers
that i grew

you'd think i'm just a simple girl
but my aspiration's
to know the world
through my own backyard

i attract butterflies
as i plant more seeds
and i love the way
my garden looks
with a few weeds

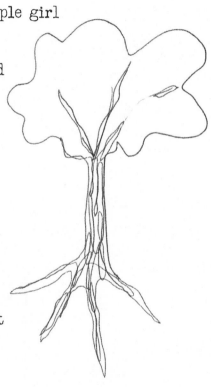

oh you see
i climb a tree
and
read

i'm learning of the secret
i'm learning of new life
i'm learning of my gift
i'm learning to fly

service, communion, awareness, acceptance,
creative existence, faith, connection,
giving, releasing, immortality

oh what it is
what it is
to be free
release
to just be
just be

waves of life
separate paths will be taken
if they need to be taken
sometimes
it's what we need
for our souls to awaken

if we could not find the beauty
in our own divine
what makes you think
it would work out fine?

restless and broken
i seem uneasy
others, they try
but they can't seem to please me

as i look back on the world so open
i know we were meant to be broken
let us float on the waves of life
let us float on the waves of life

our dreams have shifted
but have grown together
now we will make our own endeav-
ors
the word forever doesn't scare me
it's how i know that things are
meant to be

now it seems
the stars have aligned
i've got my ruler out

i can see it
this time

let us float on the waves of life
let us float on the waves of life
let us float on the waves of life
let us float on the waves of life

may we join together
abandoning our fears

and move forward
hand-in-hand

with
love, grace, and kindness.

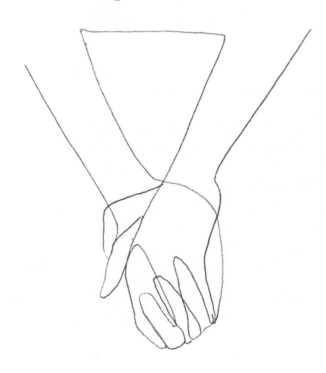

life
it's not a competition
just an opportunity to grow

the fact is
there are things you'll never think
of
and a billion things you'll never
know

you can live your life hoping
that you'll find a better way

or you can spend your life doing
and making time to play

i could dance a thousand dances
and sing a million songs

the truth is
i'll never know of all my blessings
but i can feel that i belong

imagine
i hope your imagination
is not making me into something
that i'm not

all you see are posts
you make some judgements
then throw me shade
you think i'm like that
do you babe

you think you know who i am
from the screen
from wherever you stand

and that's fine
but that's not me
it's only a reflection
of your own strengths
or your own insecurities

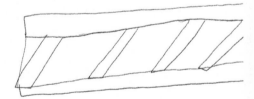

i know myself
it is all a journey
for all of us
i pray for you
i pray for us

i hope your imagination isn't taking you places
that will hurt you down the road

i hope your imagination isn't taking you places
that will hurt you down the road

limoncello
oh what have i given you
to construct your memories of me

is it something i left behind
unless i go back i'd never find
which fragments did i leave behind

do you use them
to make up your memories of me
to make up
your memories
of me

is there something you've forgotten
that i hold on to
they leave spaces
you'll soon forget

and if you were to see me again
would you recognize my face
and let go of all the fragments
would i be whole in your memory
again?

oh what have you forgotten?
what have you forgotten
in your mosaic memory of me?

oh but how can we judge

when it is truly only light

that creates and shapes

every form we've ever known

rose tinted
like blinded eyes subject to glasses
you let me see every single leaf
and i am the wind that dances through
you
you're the tree that sways to my beat

how can i take you with me?

i wore your love like glasses
and now i'm able to see your every vein

how i can i take you with me?

i treat you like ground
i lay with you
i step on you
and i'll kiss you when i'm back from sea

how can i take you with me?

you might not see it the same way i do
and i wish i could share these glasses
because it's oh so clear to me that it's you

if you do not think
that you are deserving

then how could you
ever accept

all of the 'more'
you keep asking for

think of a rainbow

light wears many shades

if you come to completely understand someone
you will not be able to help yourself
but to love them
and see love and light
in all that they do

is it our understanding that illuminates?
or our love that permits understanding?

perhaps because we see dark matter
as darkness
we will never understand it
for all we may understand and know
is light

what if
to reach understanding of anything
we are simply being called
to expand the depth
to which we are willing
to look at something
as light

daisy
you know a rich girl
never marries a poor boy
and men will beg you
to make them your toy

i'm reckless and careless
but it's what the world
wants from me

oh gatsby
please excite me
i am troubled with boredom

your smile
oh
you always look so cool

please bring out
your old uniform
and hold me close
as we beat on
boats against the current
bourne back into the past

we cannot recreate the
past
it's best a living memory
you can make of me
what you want
but you'll never
get the best of me

i'm reckless and careless
but it's what the world
wants from me

oh gatsby
oh gatsby
you delight me
with your obsession with
me

your smile
oh
i feel so adored

please bring out
your old uniform
and hold me close
as we beat on
boats against the current
bourne back into the past

so i showed this man
he had my love
while he was alive
it's not my fault
he had a dream
that was never realized

i'm reckless and careless
but it's what the world
wants from me

oh gatsby oh gatsby
you know I'll never be
sorry
so now i must leave
yes
you can't live forever
you can't live forever

so why would i live to die
you knew a rich girl
never marries a poor boy

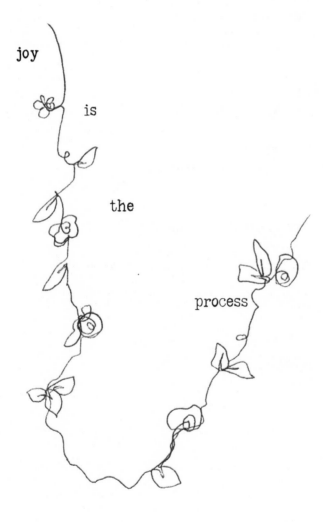

joy

is

the

process

starlight moonlight
don't fear the pain
don't fear the pain

i know this
i say this
and i try to feel the same

don't fear the night
there will always be light
in some sort of reflection

but if you cannot see the light
and darkness surrounds you
then you need to take yourself from shelter

take yourself out of your comfort

because it is only your comfort
that is blocking
the light

TBH

to be honest
you're the reason
i'm not going home

to be honest
you're the reason
i'm writing this song

to be honest
i think that
you're the one

to be honest
you're the reason
i'm coming home

to be honest
you're not the reason
i'm writing this song

to be honest
i know that
you're not the one

i was always honest

but we co-create the truth.

i am free

love comforts me

we are all divinity

LIGHT
anything can happen
anything can knock at your door
that i am sure

let yourself believe
let yourself be free
let yourself believe
in the good
that i've understood

it's all okay
you will find your way

it's all okay
sing it with me
it's all okay
i'll find my way
it'll happen someday
because i have faith
i have faith

here and now
is exactly where i'm supposed to be
and life keeps showing me how to
love more and give more
be more free
i want you all to be free with me
it's okay
it's alright
let there be love
follow the light

you need not seek perfection
as it exists in this very moment

in everything

you're going to find it someday
there is no other way

if you don't know how
just focus on the now

yeah life tends to figure itself out
just be here with me now

appreciate the little things
so much love life can bring

i'm so grateful that you're here
and that for one moment
you have no fear

i'm so grateful that you're here
and hold my hand
yes beauty, have no fear
just be with me here

there's no other way to be

i accept you as you are
let me be clear
i just want you here

let us hear each other's truths
life is so beautiful with you

d e f i n e
art
is
art
if it's from the heart

any expression you give of your soul
is a divine creation
that's beautiful

forced

let me fall in love with you
i know it's not an easy thing to do
to let me fall in love with you
you will have to look me in the eye

you make it harder still
you are unwilling to tell the truth
it's easy to see the lie
and you can't understand why

i am trying to fall in love with you
i know it's not an easy thing to do

every time i try to leave
you come and beckon me to stay
though i still try to leave
i must say i like it this way

let me fall in love with you
i know its not an easy thing to do
to let me fall in love with you
you will have to give me love too

oh if you ever tried to leave
i would never beg you to stay
i think that's why you never leave
you want to continue this play

oh but i am through with these games
it's time to raise the stakes

let me fall in love with you
i know it's not an easy thing to
do

yes you can bet
it's hard for me too.

through shadow

and　l i g h t

we take form

we all
come to find

that our
hearts

give far
better directions
than our
minds.

sometimes

we cannot open a jar

simply because
our

hands are wet

koi no yokan
from coast to
coast
i've been
you have the   and though
most   we just
beautiful   barely met
smile   i want to be
                  with you   and though
                  for awhile   you
                                  barely
                                  speak english

                                  i
                                  want to make
                                  you
                                  my love

                                  want to make
                                  you
                                  my love

five
i feel
the breeze is coming
no one else trusts
the storm warning
so i set out alone
on a new life
no one i have met
can match my stride
or harm my peace
or my pride

dead man
dead man
come alive

before i count
to the number five

one, two, three, four

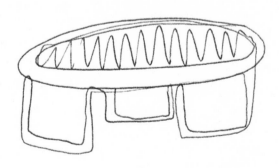

i don't believe in pathological disorders
i believe in genetic diversification
nature loves diversity
it's humanity that has trouble dealing with it

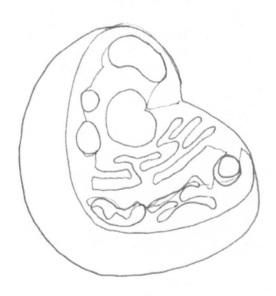

perhaps
indeed
in order to succeed
all life asks from you

is that you believe

NEVER GOODBYE
may you always have chapters
that remain unwritten
and may your book
remain unbound
life will take us
on a hell of a ride
but here
you'll always find sturdy ground

be sure to keep accepting others fully
you never know what you're missing out on
appreciate those who you hold dearly
remember a real friend will never be gone

may happiness guide you through your jour-
ney
your friends will make the trip go faster
now
you'll always have someone, don't you worry
if you're lost, love will help you out

growth in life is what gives us our luster
keep challenging yourself in new ways
clarity will work through the cluster
life is good, so keep it up for brighter days

above all stay beautiful

a beautiful mind stays open
a beautiful soul stays free
a beautiful heart stays open
and the memories stay with me
stay
stay
stay with me.

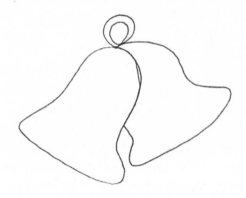

VOWS
i
love
you
now

for
the
present
is
the
only
thing
which
has

no end.

sculpture

what is chipped away
holds great significance
as it is most formative
to the shape
and defining features
of the masterpiece
that stands before you.

perhaps
we are
more like sculptures
than we realize
and what defines
our lives
is created
by what
we choose
to let go of.

strangely magical
we are somehow
outlined
by all
we have forgotten.

we   excelsior
can give
something so
beautiful to this world
j u s t need to c h a n g e the
f o u n d a t i o n that we've built
build it on trust
build it on love
build it on faith
build it on belief
in   the   g o o d
                              we
we're all h e r e
you should have   can give
n o   f e a r   something so
we're   in   this   be a u t i f u l
together forever   to this w o r l d
together forever we can open their eyes
              and change what they see
          we can hold each other's h a n d s
          we can set e a c h o t h e r free
        i w e c a n s h o w e a c h o t h e r
        c a n   w   h   o
     g i v e   w e 'r e
   the   w o r l d   m e a n t
  a new kind of peace   t o   b e
  i can help them accept
 a n d   finally r e l e a s e
i can help them pave a new path
         and reach
         d   e   e   p
         i can   do
         s o   much
         if you   do
         it with me
         we're in this
         t o g ether
         f o r e v e r
         we're in this
         t o g ether
156   f o r e v er

T R U E   LOVE?

and if love
is non-attachment

perhaps i've only
really loved
everything
that i've
forgotten.

good morning
give me a second
while i wake up
sure we can meet for coffee
just let me get out of bed

good morning
i forgot to wash my makeup
let's go grab some breakfast
i'll race you out of bed

good morning
you don't have to get up
i'll go grab my teacup and
meet you back in bed

good morning darling
you should get up
don't forget your coffee
mug
you've got a big day ahead

good morning
did you hear the baby
its fine you can sleep in
i'll get out of bed

good morning
if you don't want to get up
i'll go start the breakfast
you lie-in instead

good morning
can you believe we're alone
all our kids are full grown
and who knows what's ahead

good morning darling
what a life we've made
whatever it is
we have to do today
you can cuddle me instead

i LOVE what i've forgotten
because the lines of what i am
are defined
by what i am not
everything i've ever let go of
has shaped me into who i am today
and i love that
i love what i've forgotten
because i love who i am.

.

---

i   LOVE

---

outro

wherever you find yourself on this
journey of life: continue forward with
faith, hope, and love

you never know of the bigger picture
that your path is
drawing

xx

about the author

Walkyria Whitlock was born in Magic Valley, Idaho. She loves meditation, yoga, traveling, tea, singing, walking, swimming, long baths, truffle, and all things rose.

She stayed in Idaho until 2013 when she left to live with a friend in Fiji. Her three month stay sparked her journey around the world. She has lived in and traveled to over 29 different countries and fallen in and out 'love' too many times before finding true love in God--becoming grounded in her beliefs and finding clarity in her vision.

Author Portrait by Sara Rose Photography

Throughout her journey, she made a point of following her intuition, facing her fears, and trusting the process--putting spirit over everything. All along the way, she has been writing and singing, keeping a collection of her work through her phone recordings and in journals. This is how 'i LOVE what i've forgotten' took form. The work of God is constant.

She has a great reverence for life and is awestruck as she reflects on where she came from, where she has been, and where she is going. She hopes to inspire you to love and live fearlessly with intention.

Learn more at www.walkyriawhitlock.com.

publisher's notes

This book would not be possible without freedom of ex-
pression and the nurturing, healing, and inspirational
qualities of nature.

Forever we stand, with you, for human rights and envi-
ronmental conservation. Visit our website to see ways we
support these causes.

Our mission at Lorem Publishing House is to inspire a
greater appreciation for life through connection. We
feel our greatest connections arise through nature
and expression, which is why we forever choose to help
those causes whenever possible. We see a world united
by a respect for ourselves, each other, and the environ-
ment.

Thank you again for your support. We hope this book
inspired a greater joy for your life and inspired you
to connect with others

lorem
PUBLISHING HOUSE

poem directory

78. naive
79. rock-a-bye
80. great cost
81. how to fly
82. leo
83. nora
84. big bang
85. relativity
86. circles
87. metamorphosis
88. all things
89. Eunoia
90. hypothesis
91. relate
92. a visual spritzer
93. flavor
94. a home
95. birdie
96. no matter what
97. brokenness
98. the sea
99. friendship blessings
100. en ad
101. bang
102. breeze
103. our path
104. like clay
105. here
106. shore
107. yolo
108. ashes
110. no limit
111. all i know
112. anchored
113. objectified
114. accept
115. luna lullabies
116. light to you
117. seeing is believing
118. start to fly
119. sleep peacefully
120. empty
121. je m'en fous
122. who are you?
123. lens of love
124. enslaved
125. the secret
126. waves of life
127. hand-in-hand
128. life
129. imagine
130. limoncello
131. every form
132. rose tinted
133. more
134. rainbow
135. dark matter
136. daisy
137. joy
138. starlight moonlight
139. TBH
140. we are all divinity
141. LIGHT
142. in everything
143. life is so beautiful with you
144. define
145. forced
146. through shadow
147. hearts directions
148. we cannot open a jar
149. koi no yokan
150. five
151. disorders
152. to succeed
153. NEVER GOODBYE
154. vows
155. sculpture
156. excelsior
157. TRUE LOVE?
158. good morning
159. i LOVE what i've forgotten
160. =

Made in the USA
Las Vegas, NV
25 September 2021